Foreword

For the last 15 years I have been trying out restricted diets including low FODMAP, gluten free, dairy free and refined sugar free.

I have found recipes from many sources which cater for one restriction or another, but the real challenge came when trying to find recipes that combined to fit all the restrictions.

Having compiled my own folder of recipes, with notes and adaptations, I decided to take the plunge and create something to share with others who want to have a similar book to hand.

The aim of this book is to provide a collection of simple, tasty, easy to cook recipes that,

- are low FODMAP, gluten free, dairy free and refined sugar free; and
- cover all the meals of the day along with some snacks and treats.

The recipes are presented in a simple style with pictures of how each dish turned out when I cooked the recipe. I hope you find it helpful and enjoy eating the results.

Thanks go to my chief tasters: my husband and son.

Contents

Ingredient Options

All the ingredients used in the recipes in this book are classified as low FODMAP by the Monash University App. In some of the recipes you can choose different low FODMAP ingredients to suit individual choice. The maximum quantity per serving at which they are considered low FODMAP is shown in (...) throughout this chapter.

MILK

Almond ....(1 cup)
Coconut, can....(1/3 cup)
Hemp....................(1 cup)
Lactose free ....(1 cup)
Macadamia ....(1 cup)
Quinoa ....(1 cup)
Rice......................(¾ cup)
Soy Protein ....(1 cup)

NUTS

Brazil............................(10)
Chestnuts ....(20)
Macadamia ....(20)
Peanut........................(32)
Pecan............ (10 halves)
Pine nut .... (1 tbsp)
Tiger .... (1 handful)
Walnut .... (10 halves)

SEEDS

Caraway .... (2 tsp)
Chia .... (2 tbsp)
Flax........................ (1 tbsp)
Poppy .... (2 tbsp)
Pumpkin............... (2 tbsp)
Sesame................ (1 tbsp)
Sunflower.............. (2 tsp)

CHEESE

Mozzarella (½ cup), Feta (½ cup), plain soft goats cheese (½ cup) and Pecorino (½ cup) are low FODMAP, or soy cheese (2 slices) can be used as a low FODMAP dairy free alternative.

YOGHURT

Plain goat's yoghurt (1 tub) and plain lactose free yogurt (1 tub) are low FODMAP, or plain coconut yoghurt (1 tub) can be used as a low FODMAP dairy free alternative.

BUTTER

Butter is low FODMAP (1 tbsp), or plant and oil based spreads (1 tbsp) can be used as low FODMAP dairy free alternatives.

SPICE MIXES

Garam Masala, Curry Powder and Chinese Five Spice powder can all be low FODMAP if they only contain the mix of spices, however some brands add other ingredients such as onion and garlic, so just check the ingredients of the brand you buy to ensure it only contains the spices.

REFINED AND NATURAL SUGAR

Vanilla extract

Vanilla extract or essence (1 tbsp) contains refined sugar, so substitute with the seeds of one vanilla pod per 1 tsp to eliminate the sugar.

Dark Chocolate

Dark chocolate (30g) contains refined sugar when bought in a bar, although cocoa powder (2 heaped tsp) does not tend to contain refined sugar, just check the ingredients on the brand you buy.

You can substitute the dark chocolate bars with ones which contain an alternative sweetener (see below for options), or use dark chocolate chips (30g) instead, as many brands of dark chocolate chips do not contain refined sugar, just check the ingredients on the brand you choose.

Low FODMAP Alternative Sweeteners

Agar..(1 stick)
Coconut/Palm Sugar.................. (1 tsp)
Icing Sugar..................................(1 tbsp)
Maple Syrup ....(1 tbsp)
Rice Malt Syrup ....(1 tbsp)
Stevia....................................(2 sachets)
Sugar, Brown...............................(1 tbsp)
Sugar, Raw..................................(1 tbsp)
Sugar, White ....(1 tbsp)

FRUIT

The following list details low FODMAP fruit, and the maximum quantity per serving at which they are considered low FODMAP.

Banana, firm only................(1 medium)
Blueberry.. (20)
Clementine.........................(1 medium)
Grapes, Black............................. (1 cup)
Grapes, Green .... (1 cup)
Grapes, Red .... (1 cup)
Melon, Cantaloupe.................. (½ cup)
Melon, Honeydew.................... (½ cup)
Kiwi.. (2 small)
Lemon Juice................................ (1 tsp)
Lime Juice................................... (1 tsp)
Orange, Navel .... (1 medium)
Pineapple .... (1 cup)
Raspberry... (10)
Rhubarb .... (1 cup)
Strawberry.. (10)

VEGETABLES AND SALAD

The following list details low FODMAP vegetables and salad, and the maximum quantity per serving at which they are considered low FODMAP.

Alfalfa .... (½ cup)
Aubergine .... (½ cup)
Bamboo Shoots................... (eat freely)
Beans, Green.................................. (12)
Bean Sprouts........................ (eat freely)
Bell Green Pepper .... (½ cup)
Bell Red Pepper .... (eat freely)
Bok Choy.................................... (1 cup)
Broccoli, heads only................... (1cup)
Brussel Sprouts .... (2)
Cabbage, excluding Savoy .... (1 cup)
Carrot .... (eat freely)
Celeriac .... (½ cup)
Chard Leaves...................... (eat freely)
Chicory Leaves .... (½ cup)
Chilli, Green ....(11cm max)
Chilli, Red ....(11cm max)
Chinese Cabbage/Wombok... (1 cup)
Choy Sum .... (eat freely)
Chrysanthemum Greens .... (1 cup)
Collard Greens.................... (eat freely)
Courgette .... (½ cup)
Cucumber .... (eat freely)
Endive Leaves .... (eat freely)
Fennel Bulb .... (½ cup)
Fennel Leaves .... (½ cup)
Ginger .... (eat freely)
Kale .... (eat freely)
Kohlrabi .... (1 cup)
Leek, green tops only............... (½ cup)
Lettuce, Butter..................... (eat freely)
Lettuce, Cos .... (1 cup)
Lettuce, Iceberg .... (eat freely)
Lettuce, Radicchio .... (1 cup)
Lettuce, Red Coral .... (eat freely)
Mushroom, Oyster...................... (1 cup)
Okra .... (6)
Olives, Black......................... (eat freely)
Olives, Green....................... (eat freely)
Parsnip .... (eat freely)
Potato, not Sweet Potato .. (eat freely)
Pumpkin, Japanese .... (eat freely)
Radish .... (eat freely)
Rocket Leaves..................... (eat freely)
Seaweed............................. (eat freely)
Spaghetti Squash....................... (1 cup)
Spinach Leaves, Baby............... (1 cup)
Spring Onion, green tops......(1 bunch)
Swede .... (1 cup)
Tomato, Cherry .... (4)
Tomato, Common .... (eat freely)
Tomato, Roma .... (1 small)
Turnip .... (1 cup)
Water Chestnuts .... (½ cup)

Cooking times and Temperatures

All appliances vary. The times and temperatures given here are what I've used, but they should be treated as guidelines. Always make sure that you check your food is properly cooked through before serving it.

Measurement Equivalents

1 cup	250ml	1 tbsp	15ml	1 tsp	5ml
¾ cup	180ml	½ tbsp	15ml	½ tsp	2.5ml
⅔ cup	160ml			¼ tsp	1.25ml
½ cup	125ml				
¼ cup	60ml				

All measures are level unless otherwise specified

Granola and Overnight Oats

Granola

Oven 160°C

½ cup of each of your chosen nuts*
1 - 3 tbsp of each your chosen seeds*
2 tbsp coconut sugar
½ cup maple syrup
6 tbsp coconut oil

Blend all the nuts, seeds and coconut sugar in a food processor
Heat the coconut oil and maple syrup in a large pan
Add the nut/seed mix and stir well
Spread evenly onto a large baking tray
Bake for 20 - 25mins until golden brown
Let cool completely

* Refer to Ingredient Options on page 7

Overnight Oats, Banana Chocolate

Serves 1

½ cup gluten free oats
4 tbsp milk*
2 tsp cocoa powder*
1 banana (firm), mashed
4 tbsp plain yogurt*
2 drops of vanilla essence*
4 tsp maple syrup
1 tsp ground cinnamon
56g dark chocolate chips*

Mix all the ingredients well, put in a Kilner jar
Seal it with the lid and refrigerate overnight
* Refer to Ingredient Options on page 7

Overnight Oats, Chia

Serves 1

1 cup gluten free oats
¼ cup chia seeds
2 tsp ground cinnamon
1¼ cup milk*
2 tbsp maple syrup
1 banana (firm), sliced
½ cup blueberries
½ cup strawberries, sliced

Mix the oats, chia and cinnamon
Mix the maple syrup and milk
Then combine and stir thoroughly
Layer the oat mix and fruit in a Kilner jar
Seal it with the lid and refrigerate overnight
* Refer to Ingredient Options on page 7

Smoothies

Banana and Oat

Serves 1

1 banana (firm), chopped
1 tbsp gluten free oats
1 heaped tsp ground flax
200ml milk*
Pinch of ground cinnamon

Blend all the ingredients together

* Refer to Ingredient Options on page 7

Carrot

Serves 1

1 carrot, peeled and sliced
1 tbsp fresh lemon juice
2 tomatoes, chopped
1 tsp fresh ginger, peeled and chopped
4 ice cubes
½ cup water

Blend all the ingredients together

Lemon and Ginger

Serves 1

Few baby spinach leaves, or greens
2 mini cucumbers, chopped
1 tsp fresh ginger, peeled and chopped
1 cup of water
2 tomatoes, chopped
Juice of 1 lemon
1 tbsp chia seeds
1 cup of ice

Blend all the ingredients together

Peanut, Banana and Blueberry

Serves 1

½ banana (firm), chopped
1 tbsp peanut butter
½ cup of blueberries
¾ cup of milk*
4 - 5 ice cubes

Blend all the ingredients together

* Refer to Ingredient Options on page 7

Strawberry and Banana

Serves 1

½ banana (firm), chopped
6 strawberries, chopped
¾ glass of milk*
1 tsp maple syrup (optional)

Blend all the ingredients together

* Refer to Ingredient Options on page 7

Tomato and Cucumber

Serves 1

2 tomatoes, chopped
Pinch of salt
1 tbsp chia seeds
1 cup of ice
½ cucumber, chopped
Juice of 1 lime
Pinch of cayenne
1 cup of water

Blend all the ingredients together

Soups

Carrot and Coriander

Serves 2

2 heaped tsp ground coriander
1 tbsp tomato puree
4 carrots, peeled and diced
600ml boiling water
Seasoning to taste

Put all the ingredients in a pan
Simmer for 20mins, until carrots are soft
Blend

Carrot, Coconut and Ginger

Serves 6

8 carrots, peeled and diced
4 parsnips, peeled and diced
1 inch fresh ginger, peeled and chopped
1L boiling water
1 tsp turmeric
1 tbsp paprika
Seasoning
4 tbsp coconut milk from a can
1 tbsp apple cider vinegar

Put the vegetables, ginger, turmeric, paprika and water in a large pan, season to taste
Simmer for 20mins, until vegetables are soft
Cool slightly then add the coconut milk and apple cider vinegar
Blend

Celeriac, Carrot and Swede

Serves 4

300g carrots, peeled and diced
200g celeriac, peeled and diced
200g swede, peeled and diced
1 inch of fresh ginger, peeled and chopped
½ tsp paprika
½ tsp turmeric
Seasoning

Heat a bit of butter or oil in a large pan
Add the veg and spices, season to taste and cook for 5mins
Cover with water then simmer for 20mins, until vegetables are soft
Blend

Courgette, Potato and Cheese

Serves 4

2 baking potatoes, peeled and diced
3 courgettes, sliced
Seasoning
2 - 3 sprigs fresh chives, chopped
100g mixed grated Cheddar and Pecorino*

Simmer the potatoes in a large pan of water for 5mins
Add the courgette and chives, season to taste
Simmer for 10mins, until vegetables are soft
Remove from heat and add the cheese
Blend (add more cheese to thicken as required)

* Refer to Ingredient Options on page 7

Parsnip and Carrot

Serves 8

300g parsnips, peeled and diced
300g carrots, peeled and diced
1 tsp dried marjoram
1 tsp dried parsley
1 tsp dried thyme
Seasoning

Heat a bit of butter or oil in a large pan
Add the vegetables and herbs and cook for 5mins
Cover with water, season to taste and simmer for 15mins, until soft
Blend

Roast Red Pepper

Serves 4

½ red pepper, deseeded and diced
6 roasted red peppers (from a jar), diced
2 tbsp oil
2 tbsp tomato puree
1L water
Handful of fresh basil
Seasoning

Heat oil in a pan
Add the peppers and tomato puree, cook for 5mins
Add the water, season to taste and simmer for 10mins
Add the basil for a couple of minutes
Blend

Roast Red Pepper and Tomato

Serves 4

8 tomatoes, chopped
3 roasted red peppers (from a jar), chopped
1 tbsp tomato puree
1 tin of chopped tomatoes
Mixed herbs to taste
300ml water
2 rice cakes, crumbled
Seasoning

Put all the ingredients in a large pan, season to taste.
Simmer for 15mins, until tomatoes are soft.
Blend

Roast Vegetable

Serves 4 Oven 200°C

500g tomatoes, chopped
3 red peppers, deseeded and chopped
2 parsnips, peeled and diced
3 tbsp oil
Bunch of fresh basil
1L water
Seasoning

Put the vegetables, oil and half the basil on a non-stick roasting tray
Bake for 40mins
Boil the water and add the roast vegetables
Season to taste and simmer for 10mins
Add the rest of the basil leaves
Blend

Tomato and Coconut

Serves 4

1 tin of chopped tomatoes
4 tomatoes, chopped
1 tsp dried thyme
1 tsp chilli flakes (optional)
1 tsp paprika
1 tsp ground cumin
4 cups of water
Seasoning
1 tbsp apple cider vinegar
1 can of coconut milk, use the thick milk, discard the watery remains

Put everything except the coconut milk and vinegar in a large pan
Season to taste and simmer for 5mins
Add the vinegar and simmer for 15mins
Take off the heat, add the coconut milk
Blend

Dips

Aubergine and Red Pepper

Makes 3 ramekins

600g aubergine, diced
1 tbsp fresh lemon juice
½ tsp salt
1 roasted red pepper (from a jar), finely chopped
75ml oil
1 tbsp tomato puree
200g cherry tomatoes, halved

Place the aubergine in a colander over the sink, sprinkle with lemon and salt, leave to drain for 10mins
Heat the oil in a pan, add the aubergine, cook on low for 1 - 2 hours until soft and brown, stirring occasionally
Add the tomato puree, tomatoes and roasted pepper
Cook until tomatoes start to break down adding more oil if needed

Ginger and Carrot

Makes 2 ramekins full

6 carrots, peeled and diced
1 fennel bulb, chopped
½ tsp ground cumin
1 tbsp oil
½ tsp salt
¼ tsp cinnamon
1½ tsp fresh lemon juice
¼ tsp ground coriander
1 inch fresh ginger, peeled and chopped
Pinch of cayenne
1 tsp paprika

Boil the carrots until soft, add the fennel for 2mins
Drain and cool
Blend the carrots and fennel with the rest of the ingredients until smooth
Serve with fresh coriander

Red Pepper and Parsnip

Makes 1 ramekin

3 tbsp coconut oil
1 roasted red pepper (from a jar)
2 cups of peeled, diced parsnip
1 tbsp green spring onion tops, chopped
1 tbsp dried mixed herbs
Seasoning to taste
Extra oil

Heat the coconut oil in a pan
Add everything except the extra oil
Cook for 20mins, stirring, until the vegetables are soft
Allow to cool for 10mins
Blend, add oil as required, until smooth

Rocket and Feta

Makes 1 ramekin

2 handfuls of fresh rocket leaves
½ cup of walnuts
¼ cup of oil
Zest and juice of ½ lemon
2 tbsp of plain yoghurt*
50g Feta cheese*
Seasoning to taste

Blend all the ingredients together until smooth

* Refer to Ingredient Options on page 7

Pate

Salmon

Makes 2 ramekins full

350g salmon fillet (skinless)
1 bay leaf
1 tbsp butter or coconut oil
2 green spring onions tops, chopped
1 cup of coconut cream
1 tbsp fresh chives, chopped
1 tbsp fresh dill, chopped
¾ tsp salt
¼ tsp fresh lemon juice

Refrigerate a can of coconut milk overnight, keep the cream, discard the liquid
Put the salmon in a pan and cover with water
Add the bay leaf, simmer for 10mins, until cooked
Add the green spring onion tops for 1min
Remove the salmon and green spring onion tops
Cool fully, then blend with the rest of the ingredients until smooth

Sardine and Coconut

Makes 1 ramekin

1 tin of plain sardines, drained
1 tbsp fresh chives, chopped
2 tbsp fresh coriander leaves
2 tbsp fresh lemon juice
¾ cup coconut cream
Seasoning to taste

Refrigerate a can of coconut milk overnight,
keep the cream, discard the liquid
Blend all the ingredients together until smooth

Sardine and Mustard

Makes 2 ramekins

½ cup of butter at room temperature*
2 tins of plain sardines, drained
2 tbsp fresh chives, chopped
2 tbsp fresh parsley, chopped
1 tbsp fresh lemon juice
1 tbsp Dijon mustard
Seasoning to taste

Blend all the ingredients together until smooth

* Refer to Ingredient Options on page 7

Smoked Mackerel

Makes 1 ramekin

160g smoked mackerel, skin off
60g butter*
Juice of ½ lemon
½ tsp Dijon mustard
Ground pepper to taste

Blend all the ingredients together, until smooth

* Refer to Ingredient Options on page 7

Smoked Trout and Salmon

Makes 2 ramekins

100g smoked trout
50g smoked salmon
Juice of ½ lemon
2 tbsp fresh chives, chopped
1 tbsp dried dill
½ cup coconut milk
1 tbsp coconut oil, melted
Seasoning to taste

Blend all the ingredients together until smooth

Sunflower Seed

Makes 2 ramekins

¾ cup of sunflower seeds, soaked overnight and drained
Juice of 2 lemons
Zest of 1 lemon
1 tsp salt
1heaped tsp ground coriander
1 bunch of fresh coriander leaves

Blend all the ingredients together until smooth

Walnut

Makes 3 ramekins

2 cups of walnuts, soaked for 2 hours
2 tbsp oil
2 tbsp fresh lemon juice
2 tbsp fresh rosemary leaves
¼ cup fresh parsley leaves
2 tsp fresh thyme leaves
1 tbsp gluten free soy sauce (or to taste)

Blend all the ingredients together until smooth
(add a little water if needed)

Winter Chestnut

Makes 3 ramekins

1 tbsp oil
1 tbsp green spring onion tops, chopped
1 heaped cup Brussels sprouts, chopped
1 tbsp fresh parsley
1 loaded cup cooked chestnuts
½ tsp ground nutmeg (optional)
½ tsp ground allspice (optional)
120ml boiling water
50ml boiling water
Seasoning

Heat oil in a pan, add the sprouts and onion tops, cook for 1min
Add the parsley and 120ml boiling water, season to taste
Simmer for 10mins, until soft, then cool fully
Blend the chestnuts
Add 50ml of boiling water, blend, then rest for 5mins to absorb the water
Add the nutmeg, allspice and the sprout mix
Blend until smooth (add a little more warm water if needed)

Sides

Raita

Makes 2 ramekins

½ cup of plain yoghurt*
½ cucumber, finely diced
1 tbsp fresh coriander leaves, chopped
1 tbsp fresh chives, chopped

Mix all the ingredients together

* Refer to Ingredient Options on page 7

Roast Roots

Serves 4 Oven 200°C

3 parsnips, peeled and diced
3 carrots, peeled and diced
2 tbsp oil
Zest and juice of 1 lemon
4 - 5 sprigs of fresh thyme leaves
75g soft rindless goats cheese*
50g fresh baby spinach
Seasoning

Put the parsnips, carrots, oil, lemon juice and zest in a lined tray
Season to taste, mix well and bake for 40mins
Add the thyme leaves and mix well
Bake for 20mins, until vegetables soft
Scatter the cheese and spinach over the vegetables
Bake for a few minutes, until the cheese melting and spinach wilted

* Refer to Ingredient Options on page 7

Roasties, Crunchy New Potatoes

Serves 4 Oven 180°C

12 - 16 new potatoes
2 tbsp oil
1 tsp paprika

Boil the potatoes for 10mins then drain
Put the potatoes on a non-stick baking tray
Crush them slightly with a potato masher
Drizzle them with oil and paprika
Bake for 20mins until crispy

Roasties, Maple Parsnips

Serves 4 Oven 200°C

1kg parsnips, peeled and cut into wedges
1 tbsp oil
80ml maple syrup

Put the parsnips in a non-stick roasting tin
Pour oil and maple syrup over, mix well
Bake for 35mins until golden and tender

Roasties, Oven Chips

Serves 4 Oven 220°C

1kg potatoes, cut into wedges
1 tsp ground cumin
1 tbsp oil
2 tbsp paprika
Seasoning to taste

Mix all the ingredients well and put on a non-stick baking tray
Bake for 25mins, turning occasionally, until golden brown

Roasties, Potato Red Pepper

Serves 2 Oven 200°C

1 jar of roasted red peppers in oil, diced, retain the oil
2 large potatoes, peeled and diced
1 tbsp coriander seeds

Put the potatoes and peppers in a non-stick roasting tray
Add the oil from the pepper jar
Add the coriander seeds
Mix everything well
Bake for 1hour until the potatoes are soft
Drain any excess oil if needed to serve

Fish

Baked Cod

Serves 4 Oven 200°C

2 courgettes, diced
3 carrots, peeled and diced
1 red pepper, deseeded and diced
1 cup of pitted black olives

3 tbsp oil
Zest and juice of 1 lemon
4 cod fillets
Seasoning

Put the vegetables in an oven proof dish
Add the oil, zest and lemon juice
Season to taste and mix well
Cover with foil and bake for 15mins
Lay the fish on top of the vegetables
Cover with foil and bake for 15mins, until fish cooked through

Serve with your choice of potato*

* Refer to Ingredient Options on page 7

Baked Haddock

Serves 4 Oven 200°C

750g new potatoes
250g cherry tomatoes
70g pitted black olives
4 skinless haddock fillets

2 tbsp oil
Juice of 1 lemon
Seasoning
Handful of basil leaves to garnish

Boil potatoes for 15mins
Put the boiled potatoes in an oven proof dish
Add olives and tomatoes
Lay fish on top
Drizzle with oil and lemon juice
Season to taste
Cover loosely with foil
Bake for 15mins, until fish cooked through

Garnish with basil to serve

Baked Salmon with Lemon and Capers

Serves 4 Oven 200°C

4 salmon fillets
1 lemon, thinly sliced
1 tbsp capers

Seasoning
1 tbsp fresh thyme leaves
Oil to drizzle

Put the salmon (skin down) in a lined oven proof dish
Place the lemon slices, capers and thyme on top
Drizzle with oil and season to taste
Bake for 25mins, until fish cooked through

Serve with your choice of potato/vegetables/salad*

* Refer to Ingredient Options on page 7

Baked Salmon with Lemon and Lime

Serves 2 Oven 175°C

2 salmon fillets
2 tbsp fresh lemon juice
½ tsp dried dill

Seasoning
1 tbsp fresh chives, chopped
1 lime, cut into wedges

Put the salmon in a foil lined ovenproof dish
Drizzle with lemon juice and dill, season to taste
Wrap the foil to make a parcel around the salmon
Bake for 20mins, until salmon cooked through

Garnish with chives and lime wedges
Serve with your choice of potato/vegetables/salad*

* Refer to Ingredient Options on page 7

Baked Sea Bass with Capers

Serves 4 Oven 220ºC

4 sea bass fillets
3 tbsp oil
Zest of 1 lemon and 2tbsp juice
2 tbsp small capers

2 tsp Dijon mustard
1 tbsp water
2 tbsp flat leaf parsley leaves to garnish

Put the sea bass in a parchment lined ovenproof dish
Drizzle with oil and bake for 10mins, or until cooked through
Mix the oil, lemon zest and juice, capers, mustard and water well
Pour this over the fish and garnish with the parsley leaves

Serve with your choice of potato/vegetables/salad *

* Refer to Ingredient Options on page 7

Baked Sea Bass with Thai Sauce

Serves 2 Oven 180°C

2 sea bass fillets
3 lemongrass stalks, peeled and diced
(or 3 tsp ground lemongrass)
2 small chillies, halved and deseeded
3 tbsp oil

1 inch of fresh ginger, peeled and finely chopped
1 tsp maple syrup
2 limes, juice of one and the other cut into quarters
2 kaffir lime leaves

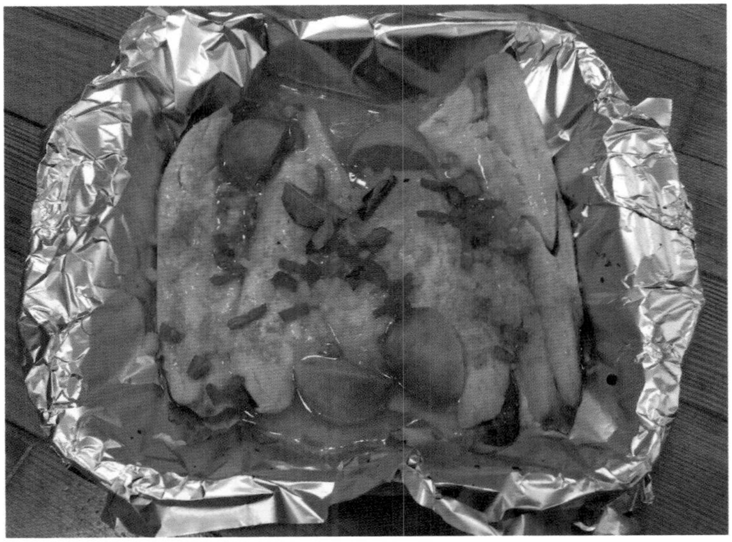

Put the lemongrass, chillies, ginger, oil, maple syrup and juice of 1 lime in a pestle and mortar, lightly crush/mix them
Put the sea bass in a foil lined ovenproof dish
Add the spice mix, 2 of the lime quarters and the kaffir lime leaves
Add the juice of the remaining 2 lime quarters
Loosely cover with foil and bake for 25mins, until fish cooked through

Serve with your choice of potato/vegetables/salad*

* Refer to Ingredient Options on page 7

Fish Curry

Serves 4

1 inch of fresh ginger, peeled and chopped
1 red chilli, deseeded and chopped
1 tbsp fresh chives, chopped
2 tomatoes, chopped
1 tbsp oil
1 tbsp low FODMAP garam masala*

1 tbsp ground cumin
1 can of coconut milk
500g white fish
2 handfuls of green beans, chopped
2 handfuls of fresh coriander leaves to garnish

Blend the ginger, chillies, chives and tomatoes into a paste
Dry fry the cumin and garam masala for a minute
Add the oil stir for a minute
Add the paste and coconut milk, simmer for 2mins
Add the fish and beans, simmer for 5mins until cooked through

Serve with rice and fresh coriander to garnish

* Refer to Ingredient Options on page 7

Maple Mustard Salmon

Serves 4 Oven 200°C

3 tbsp olive oil
3 tbsp maple syrup
3 tbsp Dijon mustard

1 tsp fresh ginger, peeled and grated
Ground pepper
4 salmon fillets

Mix the oil, maple syrup, mustard, ginger and pepper, let it stand for a few hours
Put the salmon in an oven proof dish
Add the sauce to the salmon
Bake for 15mins, until salmon cooked through

Serve with your choice of potato/vegetables/salad*

* Refer to Ingredient Options on page 7

Maple Soy Salmon

Serves 2 Oven 200ºC

2 tbsp maple syrup	1 tsp fresh ginger, peeled and grated
2 tbsp gluten free soy sauce	2 salmon fillets

Mix the maple syrup, soy sauce and ginger, let it stand for a few hours
Put the salmon in an oven proof dish
Add the sauce to the salmon
Bake for 15mins, until salmon cooked through

Serve with your choice of potato/vegetables/salad*

* Refer to Ingredient Options on page 7

Roast Sea Bass with Vegetables

Serves 2 Oven 180°C

2 sea bass fillets
300g potatoes, skin on, thinly sliced
1 red pepper, deseeded and sliced
2 tbsp oil
1 sprig of rosemary leaves

25g pitted black olives
Seasoning
½ lemon, thinly sliced into rounds
Handful of fresh basil leaves to garnish

Put the potatoes and peppers in an oven proof dish
Add oil and rosemary leaves, season to taste
Roast for 25mins, stir half way through
Put the olives, lemon and fish on top
Roast for 15mins, until fish cooked through

Garnish with basil leaves

Thai Red Curry

Serves 4

PASTE
6 red chillies, or to taste
1 tsp ground cumin
1 tsp ground coriander
1 tsp paprika
4 cm fresh ginger, peeled and chopped
2 sticks of lemon grass, peeled and chopped (or 2 tsp ground lemon grass)
2 tbsp fresh coriander leaves
2 tsp shrimp paste
1 kaffir lime leaf
Pinch of salt

CURRY
600ml coconut milk from a can
2 tbsp fish sauce
2 kaffir lime leaves
1 potato, peeled and diced
1 courgette, diced
150g green beans, chopped
800g white fish, diced
Fresh coriander to garnish

Blend all the paste ingredients together
Use half now and freeze the rest
Heat oil in a pan then add the paste and cook for 1min
Add the coconut milk, fish sauce and kaffir lime leaves and bring to a simmer
Add the potatoes, simmer for 10mins
Add the courgette and beans, simmer for 10mins
Add the fish and simmer for 10mins, until cooked through
Serve with rice, garnish with fresh coriander leaves

Thai Style Trout

Serves 4 Oven 190ºC

4 whole trout
2 sticks of lemongrass, finely chopped
(or 2 tsp ground lemongrass)

2 red chillies, deseeded and finely chopped
40g fresh coriander leaves
Juice of 1 lime

Lay out 4 large squares of foil topped with squares of parchment
Place a trout in the middle of each parchment square
Mix the lemongrass, chilli and coriander, then put it in the tout cavities
Pour lime juice over each trout
Fold up the foil and parchment to form parcels around each trout
Bake for 20mins, until cooked through

Serve with rice or "Roasties, Oven Chips" (see page 36)

Chicken

Chicken Cacciatore

Serves 4

2 tbsp oil
500g chicken breasts
1 carrot, peeled and diced
1 fennel bulb, diced
1 tbsp tomato puree
1 tin of chopped tomatoes
250ml water
1 tsp dried mixed herbs
Seasoning

Heat the oil in a pan
Add the chicken and brown it
Add the vegetables, cook for 5mins
Add the tomatoes, water, tomato puree and herbs
Season to taste and mix well
Simmer for 30mins, until chicken cooked through

Serve with your choice of potato/salad*

* Refer to Ingredient Options on page 7

Chicken Curry

Serves 2

2 chicken breasts, diced
Juice of 1 lime
100g spinach leaves
1 inch of ginger, peeled and chopped
1 red chilli, deseeded and chopped (optional)
1 tsp low FODMAP garam masala*
1 tsp turmeric
1 tsp ground cumin
1 tin of chopped tomatoes
2 tbsp oil
2 tbsp plain yoghurt*
Bunch of fresh coriander leaves
Seasoning

Marinade the chicken in the lime juice for a few minutes
Heat 1 tbsp oil in a pan, add the ginger and spices, cook for 5mins, stirring
Add the tomatoes and half the coriander, season to taste, simmer for 10mins
Blend the sauce
Heat the rest of the oil in the pan, add the chicken and brown it
Add the sauce and spinach, simmer for 10mins, until chicken cooked through
Stir in the yoghurt
Serve with rice, garnish with remaining coriander

* Refer to Ingredient Options on page 7

Chicken Mediterranean Bake

Serves 4 Oven 200ºC

1 tbsp fresh thyme leaves
4 chicken thighs
4 potatoes, peeled and diced
2 red peppers, deseeded and diced
20 pitted black olives

220g cherry tomatoes
1 tsp paprika
1 tsp ground cumin
3 tbsp oil

Put the chicken, potatoes, peppers, olives and thyme in an oven proof dish
Mix the oil, paprika and cumin, and pour over the chicken
Mix well and bake for 1hour, until the chicken cooked through

Chicken Tikka Masala

Serves 2

PASTE
3 tbsp low FODMAP garam masala*
2 tbsp fresh ginger, finely chopped
1 tbsp turmeric
Chilli Powder to taste
3 tbsp salt
1½ tsp ground cloves
1 tsp paprika powder
½ tsp cayenne pepper
½ tsp ground cumin
Fresh coriander to taste
4 green spring onions tops, chopped
Juice of 1 lemon

CURRY
200g chicken, diced
40g plain yogurt*
150ml coconut milk
100g of sieved tinned tomatoes (discard juice)
Fresh coriander to garnish

Blend all of the paste ingredients together
Use a third now and freeze the rest
Mix the paste, yoghurt and chicken and refrigerate for at least 30mins
Heat the chicken mix in a pan until cooked through
Add the sieved tomatoes and coconut milk
Simmer for 15mins until thickened a bit
Serve with rice, and garnish with coriander
* Refer to Ingredient Options on page 7

Creamy Chicken Curry

Serves 4

1 tbsp oil
450g chicken breast, diced
1½ tsp low FODMAP curry powder*
1 tsp low FODMAP garam masala*
½ tsp ground cumin
½ tsp turmeric
Pinch of cayenne pepper
Seasoning
3 potatoes, peeled and diced
1 can of coconut milk
Fresh parsley to garnish

Heat oil in a pan
Add the chicken and brown it
Meanwhile mix the spices together
Add the spice mix to the chicken, stirring to coat the chicken
Add the potato and coconut milk, season to taste
Simmer for 10mins, until chicken is cooked through
Serve with rice, garnish with parsley
* Refer to Ingredient Options on page 7

Lemon Cinnamon Chicken

Serves 4 Oven 220°C

8 chicken thighs
2 lemons, zest of one and juice of both
2 tbsp oil
750g new potatoes, cut into wedges

2 tsp ground cinnamon
2 tsp ground cumin
Seasoning

Mix the lemon juice, zest, cinnamon, cumin and oil
Put the chicken thighs in an oven proof dish
Pour the sauce over the chicken
Add the potatoes, season to taste and mix
Bake for 40mins, or until chicken cooked through

Serve with your choice of vegetables/salad*

* Refer to Ingredient Options on page 7

Maple Chili Chicken

Serves 2

1 tbsp oil
375g chicken, diced
1 red pepper, deseeded and sliced
2 green spring onions tops, chopped

½ tsp red chilli paste
3 tbsp gluten free soy sauce
1 tbsp maple syrup
Handful fresh coriander leaves

Heat oil in a pan
Add the chicken and brown it
Add the pepper, cook for a couple of minutes
Add the soy sauce, maple syrup and chilli
Cook for 5mins, until chicken cooked through, stirring to mix
Add the green spring onion tops and coriander, stir for 1min

Serve with rice or rice noodles

Mozzarella Chicken

Serves 4

4 chicken breasts
1 tbsp oil
1 fennel bulb, finely chopped
1 carrot, peeled and finely chopped
440g tin of chopped tomatoes

3 tbsp tomato puree
1½ tsp dried oregano
85g pitted black olives
250g Mozzarella, sliced*
Seasoning

Heat oil in ovenproof dish
Add the chicken and brown it
Add the vegetables for 5mins, stirring until softened
Add the tomatoes, puree, oregano and olives
Season to taste and stir
Simmer for 20mins, until chicken is cooked through
Top the chicken with the Mozzarella slices, grill for 2 - 3mins to melt the cheese

Serve with your choice of potato/salad*

* Refer to Ingredient Options on page 7

Peanut Coconut Chicken

Serves 4

3 tbsp oil
4 chicken legs, skinless

1 can coconut milk
3 tbsp peanut butter

Heat oil in a pan
Add the chicken and brown it
Cover it with water
Simmer for 40mins, stirring occasionally
Whisk together the peanut butter and coconut milk, then add to the chicken
Simmer gently for 20mins, until chicken is cooked through

Serve with rice or rice noodles

Roast Ratatouille Chicken

Serves 4 Oven 200°C

4 chicken breasts
2 red peppers, deseeded and diced
1 courgette, diced
1 aubergine, diced

4 tomatoes, halved
4 tbsp oil
A few rosemary sprigs
Seasoning

Put all the vegetables and chicken in an oven proof dish
Drizzle with oil, season to taste, add rosemary
Roast for 40mins, until chicken cooked through

Thai Green Curry

Serves 4

PASTE
6 green spring onion tops, chopped
Handful of fresh coriander leaves
2 green chillies, deseeded and chopped (or to taste)
2 stalks of lemongrass, peeled and sliced (or 2 tsp ground lemongrass)
2 tsp fresh ginger, peeled and chopped
1 tbsp fish sauce

CURRY
1 tbsp oil
4 chicken breasts, diced
1 red pepper, deseeded and sliced
1 carrot, peeled and thinly sliced
1 tbsp tinned bamboo shoots
1 can coconut milk
6 kaffir lime leaves
Juice of ½ lime

Blend all the paste ingredients together
Put oil in a pan
Add the paste, cook for 2mins
Add the chicken, cook for 2mins, stirring to coat it
Add the pepper, carrots, bamboo shoots and kaffir lime leaves and stir well
Add the coconut milk and simmer for 20mins, until chicken cooked through
Add the lime juice and stir

Serve with rice or rice noodles

Beef

Beef and Coconut Curry

Serves 4

500g beef strips
½ tsp cornflour
Ground pepper to taste
2 tbsp oil
1 inch of fresh ginger, peeled and finely chopped
1 tsp ground cumin
1 tsp ground coriander

1 tsp turmeric
1 red chilli, deseeded and finely chopped (or to taste)
1 red pepper, deseeded and chopped
1 courgette, chopped
1 can of coconut milk
Fresh coriander to garnish

Mix the beef, cornflour and ground pepper
Heat oil in a pan
Add the spices and cook for a couple of minutes
Add the beef and brown it
Add the vegetables and cook until vegetables are tender
Add the coconut milk and stir until heated through

Serve with rice, garnish with fresh coriander

Beef and Red Wine Casserole

Serves 4

1 tbsp oil
1 tbsp tapioca flour
80g diced pancetta (or streaky bacon)
650g diced beef
3 carrots, peeled and diced

1 fennel bulb, finely sliced
½ small swede, peeled and diced
Handful of fresh thyme leaves
500ml dry red wine
Seasoning

Coat the beef with the tapioca flour
Heat oil in a large pan
Add the pancetta
Add the beef and brown it
Add the vegetables and herbs, cook for a few minutes
Add the wine and season to taste
Simmer for 3 hours, until the beef is tender

Serve with your choice of potato*

* Refer to Ingredient Options on page 7

Beef Bourguignon

Serves 4

¼ cup tapioca flour
Seasoning to taste
1 tsp ground cumin
500g diced beef
1 tbsp oil
2 cups dry red wine

1 tbsp tomato puree
2 carrots, peeled and diced
2 courgettes, diced
1 bay leaf
1 tsp dried rosemary

Toss the beef in the flour, seasoning and cumin until well coated
Heat oil in a pan
Add the beef and brown it
Add the carrots and courgettes, cook for 5mins
Add the wine, bay leaf, tomato puree and rosemary
Simmer for 2 hours

Serve with rice or jacket potato

Beef Stir Fry

Serves 4

500g stir fry beef strips
1 tsp low FODMAP Chinese Five Spice*
1 red chilli, deseeded and sliced
1 tbsp oil
1 inch of fresh ginger, peeled and finely chopped
I stick of lemon grass, peeled and sliced (or1 tsp lemongrass powder)

1 handful of fresh baby spinach
1 red pepper, deseeded and sliced
6 green spring onion tops, chopped
Juice of ½ lime
2 tbsp gluten free soy sauce
1 tbsp fish sauce
1 tbsp fresh coriander to garnish

Heat oil in a pan
Add the beef
Add the Chinese Five Spice, cook for 2mins
Add the chilli, ginger and lemon grass, cook for 5mins while stirring
Add the pepper, cook for 5mins
Add the spinach and green spring onion tops
Once spinach has wilted take off the heat
Add the lime juice, soy sauce and fish sauce and stir
Serve with rice or rice noodles, garnish with fresh coriander leaves

* Refer to Ingredient Options on page 7

Creamy Beef Curry

Serves 4

1 cup of plain yoghurt*
1 tsp cornflour
2 tbsp oil
2 carrots, peeled and diced
1 fennel bulb, finely sliced
1 inch of fresh ginger, finely chopped
1 chilli, deseeded and finely chopped
500g beef, diced

1 tbsp ground coriander
1½ tsp ground cumin
½ tsp turmeric
1 tin of chopped tomatoes
¼ cup fresh coriander leaves
Seasoning
1½ tsp low FODMAP garam masala*

Mix the yoghurt and cornflour, stir until smooth and set aside
Heat oil in a pan, add the beef and brown it
Add the carrot and fennel, cook for 8mins
Add the ginger and chilli, cook for 2mins
Add the cumin and turmeric, cook for 3mins
Add the tomatoes, yoghurt mix, ground coriander
Season to taste and simmer for 25mins
Remove from heat, stir in the garam masala and fresh coriander, mix well
Serve with rice and Raita (see page 34)

* Refer to Ingredient Options on page 7

French Beef Stew

Serves 4 Oven 150°C

500g beef, diced
1 fennel bulb, diced
4 carrots, peeled and diced
2 parsnips, peeled and diced

3 potatoes, peeled and diced
500ml passata
Seasoning to taste
1 tsp dried basil

Put all except the potatoes in an oven proof dish, mix well
Cover with lid, bake for 3 hours
Add the potato and some water if required
Bake for 1hour

Pork

Mustard Pork Medallions

Serves 4

4 pork loin steaks
2 tbsp oil
2 tbsp gluten free soy sauce
1 tbsp fresh chives, chopped

Juice of 3 lemons
Ground pepper to taste
2 tsp Dijon mustard
2 tbsp water

Mix the lemon juice, pepper and pork, put in the fridge for 2 hours
Heat oil in a pan
Add the pork, and cook through, turning as required
Remove from the pan
Mix the soy sauce, chives, mustard and water, and heat for 1min
Drizzle the sauce over the pork to serve

Serve with your choice of potato/vegetables/salad*

* Refer to Ingredient Options on page 7

Pork Fillet with Mustard and Herbs

Serves 2 Oven 160°C

2 pork fillets
2 tbsp oil
150ml oil
Zest of 1 lemon

100g fresh parsley
50g fresh basil
1 tbsp Dijon mustard

Blend the 150ml oil, zest and herbs to make a paste
Heat the remaining oil in a pan
Add the pork and brown it
Transfer the pork to an oven proof dish
Bake for 30mins, until cooked through
Top with the mustard, then the paste

Serve with your choice of potato/vegetables/salad*

* Refer to Ingredient Options on page 7

Pork Pot Roast with Red Wine

Serves 5 Oven 165°C

1kg pork loin
30ml oil
3 potatoes, peeled and diced
2 carrots, peeled and diced
2 parsnips, peeled and diced
375ml dry red wine

¾ cup of fresh oregano, thyme and rosemary leaves
Seasoning to taste
30ml water
1 tbsp cornflour

Season the pork, and add half the herbs
Heat oil in an oven proof dish
Add the pork to brown it
Add half the red wine, cook for 5mins
Cover and bake for 30mins
Add the vegetables, remaining herbs and wine
Cover and bake for 1hour

Remove the pork and vegetables, leaving the wine in the pan
Mix the cornflour and water, then add to the wine
Heat while stirring, to thicken
Pour the sauce over the pork and vegetables to serve

Pork Stir Fry

Serves 2

300g pork fillet strips
1 red pepper, deseeded and cut into strips
1 carrot, peeled and cut into strips
100g tin of pineapple in juice
10g ginger, peeled and finely sliced

40g beansprouts or water chestnuts
1 green spring onion tops, chopped
2 tbsp gluten free soy sauce or white wine vinegar
1 tsp cornflour
Seasoning

Season the pork to taste
Mix the soy sauce, pineapple juice and cornflour

Heat oil in a frying pan
Add the pork and ginger, brown the pork
Add the pepper, green spring onion top and carrot, cook for 5mins
Add the beansprouts or water chestnuts and pineapple
Stir in the sauce
Mix well and let thicken

Serve with rice noodles or rice

Walnut Maple Crusted Pork

Serves 8 Oven 175°C

1kg pork tenderloin
¼ cup maple syrup
2 tbsp Dijon mustard
½ tbsp fresh thyme leaves
Seasoning
¾ cup chopped walnuts or pecans

Mix the maple syrup and mustard, season to taste
Brush the maple mix all over the pork
Roll the pork in the chopped nuts to coat it
Put the pork on a lined baking tray
Sprinkle the top with the fresh thyme leaves
Bake for 1hour, until cooked through
Cover with foil if needed

Slice to serve
Serve with your choice of potato/vegetables/salad*

* Refer to Ingredient Options on page 7

Lamb

Aromatic Lamb Warmer

Serves 6

675g lamb, diced
2 carrots, peeled and diced
1 fennel bulb, diced
1 tsp cumin seeds
1 tsp cardamom pods, bruised
2 tsp low FODMAP curry powder*

2 tbsp oil
500ml water
1 tin of chopped tomatoes
1 tin of lentils, drained and well rinsed
Large bunch of fresh mint, chopped
Seasoning

Dry fry the cumin, cardamom and curry powder for 2mins, then crush in a pestle and mortar
Mix the spices with the lamb and season to taste
Heat oil in a large casserole dish
Add the lamb and brown it
Add the vegetables, stirring for 5mins
Add the tomatoes and water
Cover and simmer for 2½ hours
Add the lentils, recover and simmer for 30mins
Add the mint just before serving or as a garnish

* Refer to Ingredient Options on page 7

Braised Lamb Shank and Root Vegetables

Serves 4 Oven 160°C

1 tbsp oil
4 lamb shanks
300ml water
Bunch of fresh thyme leaves
Bunch of fresh parsley
1 tsp fresh chives, chopped

Seasoning
4 carrots, peeled and chopped
1 fennel bulb, chopped
1 swede, peeled and diced
4 potatoes, peeled and diced

Heat the oil in a large casserole dish
Add the lamb and brown it
Add the herbs and water, season to taste
Cover with foil and a lid
Bake for 1½ hours
Add the vegetables and more water if needed
Bake for 1 hour, until lamb falling of the bone
Remove the lamb
Put the casserole on the hob and simmer to reduce the gravy

Dijon Lamb Chops

Serves 4

4 lamb chops
Seasoning
1 tbsp oil
½ cup water
½ cup dry white wine

1 tbsp Dijon mustard
2 tsp fresh lemon juice
2 tbsp butter*
3 tbsp fresh chives, chopped
1½ tsp fresh rosemary leaves, chopped

Season the chops to taste
Heat oil in a pan and cook the chops through
Put the water and wine in a separate pan
Simmer until reduced by half
Stir in the mustard and lemon juice
Simmer for 1min
Add butter and stir until melted
Add the chives and rosemary
Pour the sauce over the chops to serve
Serve with your choice of potato/vegetables/salad*

* Refer to Ingredient Options on page 7

Lamb Casserole

Serves 8

1kg diced lamb
2 tbsp oil
5 rashers of bacon, diced
1 tbsp ground coriander
1 tbsp ground cumin
1 tsp ground cardamom

½ cup dry red wine
½ cup tomato puree
1 tin of chopped tomatoes
1 tin of lentils, drained and rinsed well
2 cups of water
3 carrots, peeled and diced

Heat oil in a big casserole dish
Add the lamb and brown it
Add the bacon and brown it
Add the coriander, cumin and cardamom, stir for 1min
Add the wine, tomato puree, tomatoes, lentils and water
Simmer covered for 2 hours

Serve with your choice of potato/vegetables/salad*

* Refer to Ingredient Options on page 7

Lamb Hot Pot

Serves 4 Oven 170°C

4 thick lamb chops
1 tbsp tapioca flour
Oil
1 fennel bulb, diced
2 carrots, peeled and diced
3 parsnips, peeled and diced
Seasoning
8 sprigs of fresh rosemary
1 tbsp fresh chives, chopped
8 potatoes, peeled and sliced

Flour the lamb chops
Heat the oil in an oven proof dish
Add the floured lamb and brown it
Add the carrots and parsnips, season to taste
Cook while stirring for 5mins
Add the rosemary and just cover with water
Arrange the potato slices over the top
Cover with parchment
Cover with a lid
Bake for 1 hour
Remove the parchment and lid and bake for ½ hour to brown the potatoes

Spiced Lamb Stew

Serves 4

1 tbsp oil
Bunch of green spring onion tops, chopped
1 inch of fresh ginger, peeled and finely chopped
1 tbsp ground cumin
1 tbsp ground coriander
1 tsp fennel seeds
½ tsp turmeric
¼ tsp ground cinnamon
¼ tsp ground cloves
¼ tsp ground cardamom
¼ tsp asafoetida powder
500g diced lamb
1 tin of coconut milk
2 carrots, peeled and diced
2 courgettes, diced
1 red pepper, deseeded and diced
Handful of fresh coriander leaves
Seasoning

Heat oil in a pan
Add the ginger and green spring onion tops, cook for 2mins
Add the rest of the spices, cook for 2mins
Add the lamb, mix well and brown the lamb
Add the coconut milk
Fill the empty tin with water and add the water
Season to taste and simmer for 2 hours, stir occasionally
Add the vegetables, cook for10mins, until the vegetables are soft
Stir in the fresh coriander leaves and serve with rice

Vegetarian

Aubergine Spiced Ragu

Serves 4

2 aubergines, diced
3 tbsp oil
1 tsp fennel seeds
2 tsp ground cumin
½ tsp turmeric
Seasoning

1 tin of chopped tomatoes
1 inch of fresh ginger, peeled and finely chopped
2 chillies, deseeded and finely chopped (or to taste)
Handful of fresh coriander to garnish

Heat oil in a pan
Add the spices and cook for a few minutes
Add the aubergine
Cook for 10mins, stirring occasionally, add a drop more oil if needed
Add the tomatoes and season to taste
Cook for 10mins, add a little water if needed

Serve with rice, garnish with fresh coriander

Baked Aubergine and Mozzarella

Serves 2 Oven 180ºC

300ml passata	Oil
Handful of fresh basil leaves	125g Mozzarella, diced*
1 aubergine, thinly sliced	30g Pecorino, grated*

Heat the oil in a pan
Add the aubergine and brown it
Add the passata, simmer for 10mins
Add the basil and Mozzarella, stir for a couple of minutes
Transfer the mix to an oven proof dish
Top with grated Pecorino
Bake for 30mins

* Refer to Ingredient Options on page 7

Coconut Green Curry

Serves 4

2 tbsp coconut oil
1 inch fresh ginger, peeled and finely chopped
2 potatoes, peeled and diced
Florets from 1 broccoli clump
1 courgette, chopped
250g fresh spinach
1 can of coconut milk
1 tsp ground cumin
2 tsp turmeric
Seasoning
½ tsp chilli flakes
Juice of ½ lime
Fresh coriander to garnish

Heat the oil in a pan
Add the ginger, turmeric and cumin, cook for 2mins
Add the potato, season to taste, cook for 2mins
Add the broccoli, courgette and coconut milk
Simmer for 15mins, until potato is soft
Add the spinach, chilli flakes and lime juice
Cook until spinach wilted

Serve with rice, garnish with fresh coriander

Courgette and Saffron Risotto

Serves 4

RICE
250g basmati rice
Pinch of saffron
2 tbsp boiling water
500ml boiling water
Pinch of salt
30g butter*
Fresh basil and grated Pecorino*

VEGETABLES
1 tbsp oil
600g courgettes, diced
½ tsp paprika
1 tbsp olives
500g tomatoes, chopped
1 red chilli, deseeded and chopped
Seasoning

Mix the saffron and 2 tbsp boiling water in a small pot
Melt the butter in a pan, add the rice and salt
Stir until the butter is absorbed, don't let the rice brown
Add the saffron water and the 500ml of boiling water
Cover and simmer until liquid absorbed
Meanwhile heat oil in a pan
Add the courgettes and chilli, soften for 5mins
Add paprika, tomatoes, olives, season to taste and cook for 5mins
Combine the cooked rice and vegetables, mix well
Garnish with grated Pecorino and fresh basil to serve
* Refer to Ingredient Options on page 7

Creamy Potato Curry

Serves 4

¾ tsp coriander seeds, plus ½ tsp
¼ tsp fennel seeds
¼ tsp cumin seeds, plus ½ tsp
4 curry leaves
4 large potatoes, peeled and diced
1 tbsp oil

1 fennel bulb, diced
1 inch fresh ginger, peeled and finely chopped
1 can of coconut milk
Seasoning
Fresh coriander to garnish

Dry fry the first quantity of coriander, fennel and cumin seeds
Add the curry leaves, fry for a few minutes, do not brown
Put the dry fried spices in a pestle and mortar
Add the extra coriander and cumin seeds, then crush
Heat oil in a pan
Add the fennel and ginger, cook for a few minutes
Add the crushed spices, cook for 1min
Add the potato, cook for a few minutes
Add the coconut milk, season to taste
Cover and simmer for 30mins, until potato is soft
Serve with rice, garnish with fresh coriander

Stuffed Peppers

Serves 4 Oven 180°C

4 red peppers, deseeded and halved
1 tin of chopped tomatoes
½ cup of water
2 tbsp pine nuts
2 tbsp capers

1 tbsp fresh basil leaves
2 cups of cooked rice
1 tbsp of butter*
½ tsp ground nutmeg
1 pack of Feta cheese*

Put the tomatoes and water in an oven proof dish
Place the peppers on the tomatoes
Mix the rest of the ingredients and fill the peppers
Bake for 1 hour
Put the Feta cheese on top and put back in the oven to melt it

* Refer to Ingredient Options on page 7

Vegetable Biryani

Serves 2

RICE

¾ cup of basmati rice
1 tbsp butter*
½ tsp turmeric
¼ tsp whole coriander seeds
3 whole cardamom pods
1 cinnamon stick, broken into two
1½ cups water
Seasoning

Melt the butter in a pan
Add the spices, cook for 2mins
Add the rice, cook for 1min
Season to taste
Add the water and cover with lid
Simmer for 20mins, then take off heat

VEGETABLES

2 tbsp butter*
1½ tsp whole coriander seeds
½ tsp whole cumin seeds
5 whole cardamom pods
A handful of green beans, diced
3 new potatoes, peeled and diced
1 carrot, peeled and diced
Seasoning
⅔ cup of water

Melt the butter in a pan
Add the spices, cook for 2mins
Add the vegetables and water
Season to taste
Simmer, stirring until water almost gone and vegetables soft

Combine the rice and vegetables to serve
* Refer to Ingredient Options on page 7

Vegetable Rogan Josh

Serves 4

2 tbsp oil
1inch of fresh ginger, peeled and finely diced
1 tsp ground cumin
1 tsp ground coriander
1 tsp ground cardamom
1 tsp paprika
Pinch of cayenne pepper

3 carrots, peeled and diced
2 courgettes, diced
Handful of green beans, diced
Seasoning
1 tin of chopped tomatoes
½ cup of water
Fresh coriander to garnish

Heat oil in a pan
Add the ginger and spices, cook for 1min
Add the carrots, cook for 5mins
Add the courgette, beans, tomatoes and water
Season to taste
Cover and simmer for 20mins, until vegetables soft

Serve with rice and garnish with fresh coriander

Vegetable Stew with Dumplings

Serves 6

STEW
2 tbsp oil
1 fennel bulb, diced
1 inch fresh ginger, peeled and finely chopped
1 aubergine, diced
1 red pepper, deseeded and diced
2 carrots, peeled and diced
2 parsnips, peeled and diced
180g cooked chestnuts
1 tin of chopped tomatoes
½ cup of dry red wine
1 tbsp fresh rosemary
1 tbsp fresh thyme
1 tbsp fresh parsley
Seasoning
2 tbsp tomato puree
1 bay leaf

DUMPLINGS
120g brown rice flour
140g cornflour
1 tsp dried mixed herbs
1 tbsp baking powder
Pinch of salt
2 tbsp plain yoghurt*
250ml of milk*

While the stew is simmering, mix all the dumpling ingredients except the milk
Slowly add the milk until all the dry ingredients are incorporated
(you might not need all of the milk)

Heat oil in a large casserole dish
Add the fennel and ginger, cook for 5mins
Add the aubergine, red pepper, carrots, parsnips and chestnuts
Cook for 15mins
Add the tomatoes, puree, wine, herbs and bay leaf, season to taste
Fill the empty tomato tin with water and add the water
Simmer for 15mins

Spoon the dumpling mixture on top of the stew
Cover with a lid and simmer for 20mins - do not lift the lid
* Refer to Ingredient Options on page 7

Puddings

Cheesecake Bars

BASE

2 cups of sunflower seeds
2 tbsp of melted butter or coconut oil
4 tbsp maple syrup
Pinch of salt

Blend the sunflower seeds, then add the rest and blend until smooth
Flatten mix evenly into a lined dish, then add your choice of topping

PLAIN TOPPING

2 cups of macadamia nuts, soaked overnight then drained
3 tbsp melted coconut oil
1 tsp vanilla extract*
2 tbsp maple syrup

Blend all ingredients together, until creamy and smooth
Layer on top of the base
Drizzle top with melted chocolate (optional)

BERRY TOPPING

2 cups of macadamia nuts, soaked overnight then drained
½ cup of melted coconut oil
½ cup of berries (strawberry or raspberry or blueberry)
½ cup of maple syrup
1 tsp vanilla extract*
¾ cup of cocoa powder*

Blend all ingredients together, until creamy and smooth
Layer on top of the base

Freeze for 4 - 6 hours, cut into bars, and store in the fridge
* Refer to Ingredient Options on page 7

Chocolate Fudge Tarts

Makes 8

BASE

140g walnuts
30ml melted coconut oil
30ml maple syrup
4 tbsp cocoa powder
¼ tsp salt
½ tsp ground cinnamon

Blend the walnuts
Add the coconut oil and maple syrup, blend
Add the cocoa powder, salt and cinnamon and blend until it forms a ball
Put the walnut mix in paper cases and freeze to set them

TOPPING

1 tsp vanilla extract*
2 bananas (firm)
8 tbsp cocoa powder
4 tbsp peanut butter
4 tbsp maple syrup

Blend all the topping ingredients into a smooth paste
Layer on top of the frozen bases
Freeze for at least 30mins to set them
Store in the fridge

* Refer to Ingredient Options on page 7

Chocolate Ginger Cups

Makes 5

8 tbsp melted coconut oil
8 tbsp cocoa powder*
4 tbsp maple syrup

Pinch of salt
Crystallised ginger (ensure it only contains ginger and sugar)**

Mix together everything but the ginger
Pour a layer of the chocolate mix into paper cases
Freeze for a few minutes until set hard
Chop the ginger into small bits and sprinkle ginger bits onto frozen bases
Cover with another layer of the chocolate mix
Freeze for a few minutes, until set hard, store in fridge

* Refer to Ingredient Options on page 7

** For a refined sugar free alternative, substitute the crystallised ginger with either a slice of banana or a drop of peanut butter or a fresh raspberry (halved)

Cookies, Oat Banana Chocolate

Makes 18 Oven 175°C

4 bananas (firm), mashed
¾ cup of chopped pecan nuts
½ cup of dark chocolate chips*
1 tsp vanilla extract*
1 tsp ground cinnamon
1 cup gluten free oats
½ tsp salt

Mix all the ingredients well, add more oats if needed for a thick consistency
Spoon 18 lumps onto a lined tray then bake for 30mins
* Refer to Ingredient Options on page 7

Cookies, Oat Peanut Chocolate

Makes 12 Oven 175°C

1¾ cup of gluten free oats
¾ cup of powdered peanut butter
2 tbsp chia seeds
1 tsp ground cinnamon
¼ tsp salt
¼ cup melted coconut oil
¼ cup maple syrup
3 tbsp water
1 tsp vanilla extract*
⅔ cup dark chocolate chips*

Blend the oats, powdered peanut butter, chia, cinnamon and salt, then add the coconut oil, maple syrup, water and vanilla and blend into a sticky ball
Stir in the chocolate chips
Spoon 12 balls onto a lined tray and bake for 12mins
* Refer to Ingredient Options on page 7

Granola Berry Crumble

Serves 6 in ramekins Oven 180°C

200g raspberries
200g blueberries
1 tbsp maple syrup
2 tbsp fresh lemon juice
Zest of 1 lemon
1 tsp ground cinnamon
Granola (see page 13)

Mix everything but the granola
Put the fruit mix into ramekins
Cover the fruit with granola
Bake for 25mins, until golden

Granola Rhubarb Raspberry Pot

Makes 4

400g rhubarb, diced
1½ cups frozen raspberries
¼ cup of water
1 tsp vanilla extract*
3 tbsp maple syrup
2½ cups granola (see page 13)
2½ cups plain yoghurt*

Put the rhubarb, raspberries, water, vanilla and maple syrup in a pan
Simmer for 15mins, until fruit is soft
Cool the fruit fully
Layer the yoghurt, fruit and granola in a glass

* Refer to Ingredient Options on page 7

Granola Roasted Rhubarb Pot

Makes 4 Oven 170ºC

400g rhubarb, diced
2 tbsp maple syrup
2 tbsp fresh navel orange juice
1 tsp vanilla extract*
300ml plain yoghurt*
4 tbsp granola (see page 13)
4 tbsp maple syrup

Put the rhubarb, 2 tbsp maple syrup, orange juice and vanilla in a small oven proof dish
Roast for 15mins, until softened
Cool the fruit completely
Put the rhubarb in a glass, cover with yoghurt, top with granola, and drizzle with the remaining maple syrup

* Refer to Ingredient Options on page 7

Granola Yoghurt Berry Pot

Makes 2

4 tbsp granola (see page 13)
4 tbsp plain yoghurt*
Raspberries, blueberries and strawberries

Layer the granola then yoghurt in a glass, top with berries

* Refer to Ingredient Options on page 7

Key Lime Torte

Serves 10 - 12

BASE

1¼ cups of mixed walnuts, pecans and brazil nuts (soak overnight in water then drain)
¼ small banana, firm (optional)
½ tsp salt
2 tbsp melted coconut oil
2 tbsp maple syrup
1 tsp vanilla extract*

Blend the mixed nuts to form a coarse meal
Add the coconut oil, maple syrup, vanilla and salt, then blend
Add banana and blend until sticky
Smooth the mix down firmly in a fully lined quiche pan
Put it in the freezer for a couple of hours

TOPPING

1½ cups of macadamia nuts (soak overnight in water then drain)
½ cup almond milk
½ cup fresh lime juice
6 tbsp melted coconut oil
6 tbsp maple syrup
1 tsp vanilla extract*

Blend all the ingredients until smooth and creamy
Pour on top of the frozen base
Freeze for 2 - 3 hours, remove 5 - 10mins prior to serving
Garnish with mint leaves or crushed nuts or lime zest, store in the fridge

* Refer to Ingredient Options on page 7

Truffles, Chocolate

Makes 30

300g dark chocolate, finely chopped*
200ml coconut milk from a can
1 tbsp melted coconut oil

Put the chocolate and melted coconut oil in a bowl
Heat the coconut milk until just at boiling point
Pour the coconut milk over the chocolate mix
Gently mix until ganache formed
Cover and cool until set
Roll/shape into balls

* Refer to Ingredient Options on page 7

Truffles, Coffee Chocolate

Makes 25

200g dark chocolate*
6 tbsp fresh espresso coffee, cooled to room temperature
2½ tbsp maple syrup, at room temperature

Melt the chocolate in a bain-marie
Cool the chocolate for a few minutes
Slowly add the coffee, stirring gently (it will initially go quite sticky)
Slowly add the maple syrup, stirring gently (it will initially go quite sticky)
Cover and cool until set
Roll/shape into balls

* Refer to Ingredient Options on page 7

Truffles, Macadamia Lemon

Makes 20

150g macadamia nuts
1 tsp vanilla extract*
1 tsp lemon zest
1 tsp fresh lemon juice
2 tbsp melted coconut oil
1 tsp maple syrup

Blend all the ingredients together
Chill in the fridge for 30mins
Shape into balls

* Refer to Ingredient Options on page 7

Truffles, Whiskey Chocolate

Makes 28

250g dark chocolate, finely chopped*
80ml coconut milk from a can
45ml whiskey

Heat the coconut milk until just at boiling point
Pour the coconut milk over the chocolate
Gently stir until the chocolate has melted
Add the whiskey and stir to form the ganache
Cover and cool until set
Roll/shape into balls

* Refer to Ingredient Options on page 7

Printed in Great Britain
by Amazon

35396247R00059